1. Introduction

Artificial Intelligence (AI) has emerged as a transformative force in recent years, reshaping industries and revolutionizing how we live, work, and learn. The Instructional Design (ID) field is no exception to this trend, as AI technologies offer unprecedented opportunities to enhance the creation, delivery, and evaluation of learning experiences. This book, "Unleashing the Power of AI in Instructional Design: Transforming Learning for the Future," explores the exciting intersection of AI and ID, illuminating how instructional designers can harness the potential of AI to craft more engaging, personalized, and effective learning solutions.

As we embark on this journey, it is essential to recognize that the integration of AI in ID is not a distant dream but a present reality. From adaptive learning platforms that tailor content to individual learners' needs to intelligent tutoring systems that provide personalized feedback and support, AI is already making its mark on education and training. However, the full potential of AI in ID still needs to be explored, and it is up to instructional designers to seize the opportunities and navigate the challenges that lie ahead.

This book serves as a comprehensive guide for instructional designers, educators, trainers, and anyone interested in the future of learning. By exploring the fundamental concepts of ID, the key AI technologies relevant to the field, and the practical applications of AI across the various stages of the instructional design process, we aim to equip readers with the knowledge and tools they need to integrate AI into their work effectively.

Throughout the book, we will explore how AI can seamlessly incorporate into the established ADDIE (Analysis, Design, Development, Implementation, and Evaluation) model, enhancing each phase with powerful, data-driven insights and automation capabilities. The possibilities are vast and exciting, from leveraging machine learning algorithms to analyze learner data and inform design decisions to utilizing natural language processing to generate personalized content and assessments.

To make the content more engaging and relatable, we will introduce a recurring fictional scenario that follows the journey of an instructional designer named Sofia as she navigates the challenges and opportunities of AI-powered ID. Through Sofia's experiences, readers will gain a deeper understanding of how AI can be applied in real-world contexts and will be inspired to think creatively about the potential of AI in their work.

In addition to exploring the practical applications of AI in ID, this book also tackles the ethical considerations and challenges that arise when integrating AI into the learning landscape. We will discuss issues such as data privacy, algorithmic bias, and the importance of human oversight in AI-driven instructional design, providing readers with a balanced and informed perspective on the responsible use of AI in education.

As we look to the future, AI will play an increasingly crucial role in shaping how we design, deliver, and experience learning. By embracing the power of AI and actively participating in its development and implementation, instructional designers can create transformative learning experiences that empower learners and drive positive change.

So, whether you are a seasoned instructional designer looking to stay ahead of the curve, an educator eager to explore new frontiers in learning, or simply someone curious about the future of education, this book is for you. Join us on this exciting journey as we uncover the boundless potential of AI in instructional design and discover how, together, we can revolutionize learning for generations to come.

2. The Fundamentals of Instructional Design

Before we delve into the exciting world of AI and its applications in instructional design, it is essential to establish a strong foundation in the fundamental concepts and theories that underpin the field. This chapter will provide an overview of the basic principles, models, and challenges that shape instructional design, setting the stage for exploring how AI can enhance and transform the ID process.

At its core, instructional design systematically creates compelling, engaging, and efficient learning experiences. It draws upon a rich tapestry of learning theories, cognitive science principles, and empirical research to inform the design and development of instructional materials, activities, and assessments. From the behavioral theories of Skinner and Thorndike to the cognitive models of Piaget and Vygotsky, instructional designers have a wealth of knowledge to draw upon as they craft learning solutions that meet the diverse needs of learners.

One of the foundational frameworks in instructional design is Bloom's Taxonomy, which provides a hierarchical classification of learning objectives based on cognitive complexity. By aligning instructional content and assessments with the various levels of Bloom's Taxonomy, from remembering and understanding to analyzing and creating, instructional designers can ensure that learners are challenged and supported in their cognitive development.

Another critical consideration in instructional design is the recognition of individual differences among learners. Factors such as prior knowledge, learning styles, motivation, and cultural background can significantly impact the effectiveness of instruction. Instructional designers must be attuned to these diverse learner characteristics and employ differentiated instruction, adaptive learning, and culturally responsive design strategies to create inclusive and equitable learning experiences.

To illustrate these concepts in action, let's introduce our fictional instructional designer, Sofia. Sofia is a passionate and creative professional who recently joined a leading e-learning company. As she takes on her first project, designing a course on digital marketing for working professionals, she quickly realizes the importance of grounding her design decisions in the principles of instructional design.

Sofia begins by thoroughly analyzing her target audience, using surveys and interviews to gather data on their prior knowledge, learning preferences, and motivations. She discovers that her learners come from diverse backgrounds with varying levels of experience in marketing and technology. Armed with this information, Sofia begins to map out her instructional strategy, leveraging Bloom's Taxonomy to create a sequence of learning objectives that gradually build complexity and challenge.

As Sofia progresses through the design process, she encounters challenges that are all too familiar to instructional designers. From navigating the competing demands of stakeholders to ensuring the accessibility and usability of her learning materials, Sofia must draw upon her expertise and creativity to find practical solutions. She also recognizes the importance of collaboration, working closely with subject matter experts, graphic designers, and developers to bring her vision to life.

Throughout her journey, Sofia remains grounded in the fundamentals of instructional design, using empirical research and proven models to guide her decision-making. She understands that effective instruction is about delivering content and creating meaningful, engaging, and transformative learning experiences that empower learners to reach their full potential.

As we explore AI in instructional design, we will see how Sofia and other instructional designers can leverage the power of AI to enhance and streamline their work, from automating routine tasks to generating personalized learning paths. No matter how sophisticated the technology becomes, the fundamentals of instructional design will always remain at the heart of effective learning solutions. By combining the art and science of ID with the transformative potential of AI, instructional designers like Sofia are poised to create a new era of learning that is more engaging, efficient, and effective than ever before.

3. AI and Its Applications in Instructional Design

Artificial Intelligence (AI) is a rapidly evolving field with immense potential for transforming instructional design. From chatbots and virtual assistants to adaptive learning platforms and predictive analytics, AI technologies are already making their mark on the educational landscape. This chapter will explore the key AI technologies relevant to instructional design. We will delve into their practical applications, illustrating how they can be leveraged to create more personalized, engaging, and compelling learning experiences.

One of the most promising applications of AI in instructional design is machine learning (ML). ML algorithms can analyze vast amounts of learner data, such as assessment scores, engagement metrics, and behavioral patterns, to identify trends and insights that can inform the design of instructional content and strategies. A powerful tool that enhances the capabilities of ML in instructional design is the Experience API (xAPI), also known as Tin Can API.

xAPI is a specification for learning technology that enables the capture and sharing of data about learners' experiences, both online and offline. By tracking learner activities such as reading an article, watching a video, or attending a workshop, xAPI provides a rich, comprehensive picture of learner engagement and performance. When combined with ML algorithms, xAPI data can generate highly personalized learning experiences that adapt to each learner's unique needs and preferences.

Let's return to our fictional instructional designer, Sofia, to illustrate the power of ML and xAPI in action. As she continues to develop her digital marketing course, Sofia integrates an ML-powered adaptive learning platform that leverages xAPI data to dynamically adjust the content and pacing of the course based on each learner's performance and engagement. The platform uses xAPI to track many learner activities, from completing online modules and assessments to participating in discussion forums and real-world projects.

As learners interact with the course, the ML algorithms analyze the xAPI data in real time, identifying patterns and correlations that provide insights into learner behavior and performance. For example, the platform might discover that learners who actively participate in discussion forums have higher engagement and knowledge retention levels than those who don't. Based on this insight, Sofia designs discussion prompts and collaborative activities to encourage all learners to share their experiences and insights, fostering community and enhancing the learning experience.

The combination of ML and xAPI enables the platform to provide highly targeted feedback and recommendations to individual learners. For example, suppose a learner consistently needs help with a particular concept or skill. In that case, the platform can automatically suggest additional resources, such as video tutorials or practice exercises tailored to their specific learning needs. By leveraging the granular data captured by xAPI, the ML algorithms can ensure that each learner receives the support and guidance they need to succeed.

Another key AI technology with significant potential for instructional design is natural language processing (NLP). NLP algorithms can analyze and interpret human language, enabling the development of chatbots, virtual assistants, and automated feedback systems that provide learners with personalized support and guidance. When combined with xAPI data, NLP-powered tools can provide even more targeted and contextually relevant assistance to learners.

In her digital marketing course, she implemented an NLP-powered virtual assistant integrated with the xAPI-enabled learning platform. The assistant, named "MarketingMate," can access the wealth of data captured by xAPI to provide personalized guidance and support to learners. For example, suppose a learner asks MarketingMate for help with a specific topic. In that case, the assistant can analyze the learner's past interactions with related content, as captured by xAPI, and provide targeted recommendations based on their unique learning history.

As Sofia and her colleagues continue exploring the potential of AI and xAPI in instructional design, they are excited by the possibilities they offer to create genuinely personalized and adaptive learning experiences. By leveraging the granular data captured by xAPI and the predictive power of ML algorithms, instructional designers can gain unprecedented insights into learner behavior and performance, enabling them to design learning experiences tailored to each learner's unique needs and preferences.

Of course, using AI and xAPI in instructional design raises important considerations around data privacy, security, and ethics. As instructional designers collect and leverage increasingly detailed data about learners' activities and experiences, they must diligently ensure that this data is used responsibly and transparently, with the learner's best interests always at the forefront.

Despite these challenges, the combination of AI and xAPI represents a powerful tool for instructional designers seeking to create more engaging, effective, and personalized learning experiences. As Sofia and her colleagues continue to push the boundaries of what is possible with these technologies, they are paving the way for a new era of instructional design—where every learner can receive the support, guidance, and opportunities they need to reach their full potential.

4. Enhancing the ADDIE Model with AI

The ADDIE (Analysis, Design, Development, Implementation, and Evaluation) model has long been a staple of instructional design, providing a structured, systematic approach to creating practical learning experiences. However, with the rapid advancement of artificial intelligence technologies, instructional designers can now enhance and streamline the ADDIE process in exciting new ways. In this chapter, we will explore how AI can be integrated into each phase of the ADDIE model, using fictional case studies and dialogues to illustrate this approach's potential benefits and challenges.

Let's return to our fictional instructional designer, Sofia, as she embarks on a new project: creating a comprehensive onboarding program for her company's sales team. Faced with the challenge of designing an engaging and effective program, Sofia leveraged AI technologies to support her work at each stage of the ADDIE process.

In the Analysis phase, Sofia begins by gathering data on the sales team's current knowledge, skills, and performance gaps. Rather than relying solely on traditional methods like surveys and interviews, she uses an AI-powered learning analytics platform to analyze data from the company's CRM system and other relevant sources. The platform uses machine learning algorithms to identify patterns and correlations in the data, providing Sofia with valuable insights into the team's strengths, weaknesses, and learning needs.

Armed with this information, Sofia moves on to the Design phase, where she begins to map out the structure and content of the onboarding program. To ensure that the program is aligned with best practices in adult learning theory and instructional design, Sofia collaborates with an AI-powered instructional design assistant. The assistant, trained on a vast dataset of successful learning programs, provides Sofia with personalized recommendations and suggestions for designing engaging, realistic learning experiences.

As Sofia and the AI assistant work together to design the program, they engage in a dialogue highlighting this approach's potential benefits and challenges. While the assistant's recommendations are grounded in data and best practices, Sofia recognizes the importance of bringing her expertise and creativity to the process. She challenges the assistant's suggestions when necessary, ensuring the final design is tailored to her organization's unique needs and context.

With the design in place, Sofia moves on to the Development phase, where she begins creating the learning content and materials for the onboarding program. Once again, she leverages AI technologies to streamline and enhance this process. Sofia can quickly generate high-quality, engaging learning content tailored to her learners' needs and preferences using an AI-powered content creation tool. The tool uses natural language processing and machine learning algorithms to analyze existing content and generate new materials optimized for learning outcomes.

As Sofia works with the AI-powered content creation tool, she encounters a challenge highlighting the importance of human oversight and judgment in using AI. While the tool can generate content quickly and efficiently, Sofia realizes that some of the generated materials need to be fully aligned with her company's brand voice and values. She works closely with the tool to refine and adjust the content, ensuring that it meets the highest standards of quality and relevance.

Moving on to the Implementation phase, Sofia uses an AI-powered adaptive learning platform to deliver the onboarding program to the sales team. The platform uses machine learning algorithms to continuously analyze learner data and adapt the content and pacing of the program in real time, providing each learner with a personalized, optimized learning experience.

As the sales team engages with the onboarding program, Sofia monitors their progress and performance using the adaptive learning platform's analytics dashboard. The dashboard provides her with real-time insights into learner engagement, completion rates, and mastery of critical concepts, allowing her to identify areas for improvement and make data-driven decisions about the program's effectiveness.

Finally, in the Evaluation phase, Sofia uses AI-powered assessment and feedback tools to gather data on the impact of the onboarding program on the sales team's performance. The tools use natural language processing and machine learning algorithms to analyze learner responses and provide personalized, actionable feedback and recommendations for improvement.

As Sofia reflects on the success of the onboarding program and the role that AI technologies played in its development and delivery, she is excited by the potential for these tools to transform the way instructional designers work. By leveraging AI to support and enhance each phase of the ADDIE model, instructional designers like Sofia can create learning experiences that are more engaging, effective, and personalized than ever before.

However, Sofia also recognizes the importance of approaching AI in instructional design with a critical eye and a commitment to human oversight and judgment. While AI technologies can provide valuable insights and efficiencies, they are tools skilled instructional designers must wield with care and expertise. By balancing the power of AI with the creativity and wisdom of human designers, Sofia believes that the field of instructional design can continue to evolve and thrive in the years to come.

As Sofia looks to the future, she is excited to continue exploring AI's potential in her work and sharing her experiences and insights with her colleagues and the broader instructional design community. Through case studies, dialogues, and hands-on experimentation, she hopes to inspire and empower other instructional designers to harness AI's power to create transformative learning experiences.

5. AI-Assisted Instructional Design Products

Developing high-quality, effective learning products is a critical component of success in instructional design. From learning objectives and assessment strategies to instructional materials and performance support tools, instructional designers must create a wide range of products that help learners achieve their goals. In this chapter, we will explore how AI technologies can assist in developing and optimizing these products, using future-focused vignettes to illustrate the exciting possibilities ahead.

Imagine a future where instructional designers can access AI-powered tools to help them create and refine learning products with unprecedented speed and precision. These tools, which leverage machine learning, natural language processing, and other advanced technologies, can analyze vast amounts of learner behavior and performance data, providing designers with real-time insights and recommendations for optimizing their products.

One such tool is an AI-powered learning objective generator that can help instructional designers create clear, measurable, and aligned learning objectives for their courses and programs. The generator analyzes learner performance and engagement data and information on the specific skills and competencies required for success in a given domain. Using this data, the generator can suggest learning objectives optimized for learner success and aligned with industry standards and best practices.

For example, let's imagine that our fictional instructional designer, Sofia, is tasked with creating a new course on data analytics for business professionals. Using the AI-powered learning objective generator, Sofia inputs information on the target audience, the desired learning outcomes, and the specific skills and knowledge learners will need to acquire. The generator then analyzes this information and data on learner performance in similar courses. It suggests a set of learning objectives that are clear, measurable, and aligned with the needs of the business community.

Another AI-powered tool that can assist instructional designers in creating effective learning products is an intelligent assessment generator. This tool uses machine learning algorithms to develop assessments tailored to individual learners' needs and abilities. By analyzing learner performance and engagement data, the tool can identify areas where learners may struggle and suggest targeted assessment items to help them build their skills and knowledge.

For example, imagine Sofia is creating an assessment for her data analytics course. Using the intelligent assessment generator, she inputs information on the course's learning objectives, desired outcomes, and data on learner performance in previous course iterations. The generator then creates a set of assessment items tailored to each learner's specific needs, providing targeted feedback and recommendations for improvement.

As Sofia works with these AI-powered tools to create and refine her learning products, she is excited by the possibilities they offer for personalized, adaptive learning. By leveraging the power of AI to create learning objectives, instructional materials, and assessments optimized for each learner, instructional designers like Sofia can create genuinely transformative learning experiences that help learners achieve their full potential.

However, Sofia also recognizes the importance of human judgment and expertise in using these tools. While AI can provide valuable insights and recommendations, instructional designers must interpret and apply this information appropriately for their specific context and audience. By combining the power of AI with the creativity and wisdom of human designers, instructional designers can create learning products that are both effective and engaging.

Looking to the future, Sofia can envision a world where AI-powered tools are even more sophisticated and integrated into the instructional design process. For example, she imagines a future where virtual reality and augmented reality technologies are combined with AI to create immersive, adaptive learning experiences that can respond to learners' needs and preferences in real time. She also envisions a future where AI-powered tools can help instructional designers collaborate more effectively, sharing insights and best practices across disciplines and industries.

As Sofia reflects on AI's potential to transform the field of instructional design, she is excited by the opportunities ahead. By staying up-to-date with the latest developments in AI and other advanced technologies and approaching these tools with a critical eye and a commitment to human judgment and expertise, instructional designers like Sofia can continue to push the boundaries of what is possible in creating effective, engaging learning products. Their work can help learners worldwide acquire the skills and knowledge they need to succeed in an ever-changing world.

6. Addressing the Challenges and Concerns of AI in Instructional Design

As the field of instructional design continues to evolve and embrace the potential of artificial intelligence, it is crucial to address the various challenges and concerns that arise with integrating AI technologies. While AI offers many exciting opportunities for enhancing and transforming instructional design, it also presents a range of ethical, social, and practical considerations that must be carefully navigated. This chapter will explore some key challenges and concerns related to AI in instructional design. We will use specific examples and best practices to illustrate responsible and practical implementation strategies.

One of the primary concerns related to AI in instructional design is the issue of algorithmic bias. AI systems are only as unbiased as the data they are trained on and the humans who design them. If the data used to train AI algorithms is biased or unrepresentative of the diverse learner population, the resulting AI system may perpetuate or amplify existing inequities and discrimination. This concern is particularly relevant in instructional design, where AI technologies can significantly impact learners' access to and success in educational opportunities.

For example, let's consider a scenario where an AI-powered adaptive learning system personalizes learning pathways for students in an extensive introductory physics course. The system uses machine learning algorithms to analyze student performance and engagement data and recommend specific learning resources and activities for each student based on their needs and abilities. However, upon closer examination, it becomes clear that the data used to train the system is heavily skewed towards a particular demographic group, leading to less effective or appropriate recommendations for students from other backgrounds.

To mitigate the risk of algorithmic bias, instructional designers must take proactive steps to ensure that the data used to train AI systems is diverse, representative, and free from historical biases. This may involve intentional efforts to collect and curate data from underrepresented learner groups and ongoing monitoring and testing of AI systems for potential biases. Instructional designers should also prioritize transparency in developing and using AI technologies, providing clear information to learners and stakeholders about how data is collected, used, and protected.

Another significant concern related to AI in instructional design is the issue of data privacy and security. As AI technologies become more prevalent in educational settings, there is a growing risk of learner data being accessed, used, or disclosed without proper authorization or consent. This concern is particularly acute in instructional design, where AI systems may collect and analyze sensitive data about learners' academic performance, personal characteristics, and learning behaviors.

To illustrate this concern, imagine an instructional designer using an AI-powered tool to analyze data from a learning management system (LMS) to identify patterns and insights related to learner engagement and performance. The tool uses natural language processing and machine learning algorithms to analyze data from discussion forums, assignment submissions, and other learner activities. However, the instructional designer soon discovers that the tool collects and stores data in ways that could be more fully transparent and secure, potentially exposing learners' personal information to unauthorized access or use.

To address data privacy and security concerns, instructional designers must prioritize developing and implementing robust data governance policies and practices. This may involve working closely with IT professionals and other stakeholders to ensure that data is collected, stored, and used in ways that comply with relevant laws and regulations and prioritize protecting learner privacy. Instructional designers should also be transparent with learners about how their data is being used and provide precise mechanisms for learners to access, correct, and delete their personal information as needed.

In addition to algorithmic bias and data privacy concerns, the use of AI in instructional design also raises important questions about the role and expertise of human designers. As AI technologies become more sophisticated and capable of automating certain aspects of the instructional design process, there is a risk that the critical skills and judgment of human designers may be diminished or undervalued. Instructional designers must recognize that while AI can provide valuable support and efficiencies, it cannot replace the creativity, empathy, and contextual understanding that human designers bring to the table.

For example, let's consider a scenario where an instructional designer uses an AI-powered content creation tool to develop a series of interactive simulations for a safety training program. The tool uses machine learning algorithms to generate realistic scenarios and decision points based on data from past safety incidents and best practices in the field. However, as the instructional designer reviews the generated content, they realize that some scenarios need to account for the organization's unique culture and context fully and may not effectively promote the desired behavior changes among employees.

In this scenario, the instructional designer's expertise and judgment are essential for ensuring that the AI-generated content is appropriately tailored and contextualized for the organization's specific needs and goals. By bringing a critical eye and a deep understanding of the learner population and organizational context, the instructional designer can work collaboratively with the AI tool to refine and optimize the content for maximum impact and relevance.

As the field of instructional design continues to grapple with the challenges and concerns related to AI, practitioners need to stay informed and engaged in ongoing conversations and best practices.

This may involve participating in professional development opportunities, such as workshops and conferences focused on ethical and responsible AI development, and collaborating with colleagues and stakeholders to develop shared guidelines and frameworks for using AI in instructional design.

Ultimately, the successful integration of AI in instructional design will require a commitment to ongoing reflection, dialogue, and iteration. By approaching AI with a critical eye and a dedication to human-centered values and practices, instructional designers can harness the power of these technologies to create more effective, engaging, and equitable learning experiences for all.

7. Fictional Case Studies: AI in Action

In the rapidly evolving landscape of instructional design, integrating artificial intelligence is no longer a distant prospect but a present reality. As AI technologies advance and mature, instructional designers increasingly explore leveraging these powerful tools to create more engaging, effective, and personalized learning experiences. In this chapter, we will present a series of fictional case studies that showcase the potential diverse applications of AI in instructional design across various industries and contexts. Each case study will follow the journey of an instructional designer as they navigate the challenges and opportunities of AI-powered design, illustrating the transformative potential of these technologies in action.

Case Study 1: Personalized Learning in Higher Education

Meet Emily, an instructional designer at a large public university. Emily has been tasked with developing an introductory psychology course serving a diverse population of over 1,000 students each semester. With the challenge of creating a course that can effectively engage and support learners with various backgrounds, abilities, and learning preferences, Emily decided to explore using AI-powered personalized learning technologies.

Working closely with a team of data scientists and software developers, Emily implements an adaptive learning platform that uses machine learning algorithms to continually assess and adjust to each learner's unique needs and progress. The platform integrates with the university's learning management system, collecting data on learners' interactions with course materials, assessments, and activities. This data is then used to generate personalized learning paths for each student, providing targeted recommendations for resources, activities, and support based on their strengths, weaknesses, and goals.

As the course launches and learners engage with the platform, Emily monitors the system's performance and impact using AI-powered analytics tools. She can track learner progress in real time, identifying areas where students may struggle and intervening with targeted support and resources. The platform also provides insights into the effectiveness of different instructional strategies and materials, allowing Emily to optimize and refine the course continuously based on data-driven insights.

The results of the AI-powered personalized learning approach are impressive. Compared to previous semesters, learners in the course demonstrated higher engagement, persistence, and achievement, with fewer students falling behind or dropping out. The adaptive platform effectively supports learners with diverse needs and backgrounds, providing a more equitable and inclusive learning experience. Encouraged by these outcomes, Emily begins to explore ways to scale the use of personalized learning technologies across other courses and programs at the university.

Case Study 2: AI-Assisted Training in the Automotive Industry

Next, we turn to the story of Mark, an instructional designer working for a major automotive manufacturer. Mark has been asked to develop a training program for the company's network of dealership technicians, focused on the diagnosis and repair of a new line of electric vehicles. With the rapid pace of technological change in the automotive industry, Mark recognizes the need for a training solution to keep pace with the evolving skills and knowledge required of technicians.

To address this challenge, Mark decides to leverage the power of AI-assisted training technologies. He works with a team of subject matter experts and AI developers to create a virtual training platform that combines immersive, interactive simulations with intelligent tutoring and performance support. The platform uses computer vision and natural language processing technologies to provide technicians with realistic, hands-on practice in diagnosing and repairing virtual vehicle systems. As technicians work through the simulations, the AI-powered tutoring system provides real-time feedback and guidance, adapting to each learner's performance and progress.

The virtual training platform is supplemented by a mobile performance support app that technicians can access on the job. The app uses AI algorithms to provide technicians with just-in-time information and guidance based on the specific vehicle and problem they are working on. The app can recognize vehicle components using computer vision, provide step-by-step repair instructions, and connect technicians with remote experts for real-time support and collaboration.

As the training program rolls out to dealerships nationwide, Mark monitors its impact and effectiveness using AI-powered learning analytics tools. He can track technician performance and engagement, identifying areas where additional training or support may be needed. The data also provides valuable insights into the real-world challenges and scenarios that technicians encounter in the field, allowing Mark to update and optimize the training content and simulations continuously.

The AI-assisted training program has proven to be a significant success for automotive manufacturers. Technicians rapidly develop the skills and knowledge to diagnose and repair new electric vehicles effectively, reducing errors and improving customer satisfaction. The virtual simulations and mobile performance support app also help to reduce training costs and time to proficiency, allowing the manufacturer to scale the program quickly and efficiently.

Case Study 3: Adaptive Learning in Corporate Compliance Training

Our final case study focuses on the work of Sarah, an instructional designer at a global financial services firm. Sarah has been asked to develop a compliance training program for the company's employees, focused on anti-money laundering (AML) regulations and best practices. With a diverse workforce spread across multiple countries and business units, Sarah faces the challenge of creating a training program that can effectively engage and educate all employees while ensuring consistent and comprehensive coverage of the complex regulatory landscape.

To meet this challenge, Sarah decided to implement an adaptive learning platform that can personalize the training experience for each employee based on their role, location, and prior knowledge. The platform uses machine learning algorithms to assess employees' existing knowledge and skills related to AML regulations. Then, it generates customized learning paths focusing on the areas where each employee needs the most support and development.

The adaptive learning platform is designed to be highly engaging and interactive. It incorporates multimedia content, simulations, and real-world scenarios to help employees apply their learning. The platform also includes gamification elements, such as points, badges, and leaderboards, to motivate and incentivize employees to complete the training and demonstrate their mastery of the material.

As employees progress through the training, the adaptive learning platform collects data on their performance and engagement. This data provides targeted feedback and recommendations for additional learning and practice and identifies areas where the training content or assessments may need to be refined or updated. Sarah also uses the data to generate reports and dashboards for company leaders, providing visibility into the overall effectiveness and impact of the compliance training program.

The adaptive learning approach effectively ensures that all employees receive the necessary training and support to comply with AML regulations. The personalized learning paths and engaging content help increase employee motivation and completion rates. At the same time, the data-driven insights allow Sarah and her team to optimize and improve the training continuously. The success of the AML compliance training program also inspires other departments within the company to explore the use of adaptive learning technologies for their own training and development initiatives.

These fictional case studies illustrate just a few of the many ways that AI technologies are transforming the field of instructional design. By leveraging the power of machine learning, natural language processing, computer vision, and other AI tools, instructional designers can create learning experiences that are more personalized, engaging, and effective than ever before. As these technologies continue to evolve and mature, the possibilities for AI-powered instructional design are endless, limited only by the creativity and vision of the designers who wield them.

8. Future Trends and Opportunities

As we've seen throughout this book, the integration of artificial intelligence in instructional design is already transforming how we create, deliver, and evaluate learning experiences. However, the story of AI in instructional design is just beginning, with a wealth of exciting trends and opportunities on the horizon. In this chapter, we'll explore some of the critical developments and possibilities shaping the future of AI-powered instructional design and consider the implications for learners, educators, and instructional designers alike.

One of the most significant trends in AI and instructional design is the growing emphasis on personalized and adaptive learning experiences. As AI technologies become more sophisticated and data-rich, instructional designers will have unprecedented opportunities to create learning experiences tailored to each learner's unique needs, preferences, and goals. This could involve using AI-powered recommendation engines that suggest personalized learning resources and activities based on a learner's past performance and interests or adaptive assessments that dynamically adjust the difficulty and focus of questions based on a learner's real-time responses.

For example, imagine a future learning platform that uses AI to create a personalized "learning journey" for each user, considering their existing knowledge and skills, desired learning outcomes, and preferred learning style. The platform could use machine learning algorithms to continually analyze the learner's interactions with content and assessments and adapt the learning path in real time to ensure that each learner is challenged and supported at the right level.

Another key trend in AI and instructional design is the growing use of natural language interfaces and conversational agents. As chatbots and virtual assistants become more sophisticated and human-like, instructional designers will have new opportunities to create engaging, interactive learning experiences that feel more like natural conversations than traditional e-learning modules. Learners could interact with AI-powered tutors or coaches that provide personalized feedback, guidance, and support throughout the learning journey, using natural language processing to understand and respond to learners' questions and needs.

For instance, consider a scenario where a learner works through a complex technical training program and encounters a concept that they find particularly challenging. Rather than struggling through dense documentation or searching for help online, the learner could ask their AI-powered tutor for assistance, using natural language to describe their question or problem. The tutor could then provide a tailored explanation or demonstration, drawing on a vast knowledge base of expert content and real-world examples to help the learner grasp and apply the concept in practice.

Using AI in instructional design will likely transform how we approach assessment and evaluation. As AI-powered analytics tools become more advanced and integrated with learning platforms, instructional designers will have access to real-time, granular data on learner performance and engagement. This could enable designers to create more authentic, performance-based assessments that measure learners' ability to apply knowledge and skills in real-world contexts rather than simply testing recall or comprehension.

Moreover, AI-powered evaluation tools could provide instructional designers with unprecedented insights into the effectiveness and impact of their learning interventions. By analyzing data on learner outcomes, behavior, and feedback, designers could identify areas for improvement and optimization and make data-driven decisions about refining and enhancing their instructional strategies over time.

As a concrete example, imagine a corporate training program that uses AI to track and analyze employees' job performance who have completed a particular course or certification. The AI system could identify correlations between specific learning activities or assessments and improved job performance, helping instructional designers focus on the most impactful and relevant content and experiences.

Of course, the increasing use of AI in instructional design also raises important ethical and social considerations. As AI systems become more autonomous and influential in shaping learning experiences, there is a risk that they could perpetuate or amplify existing biases and inequities in education. Instructional designers must be proactive in ensuring that AI-powered learning experiences are designed with fairness, transparency, and accountability in mind and that they prioritize the needs and well-being of all learners.

One way to address these concerns is by developing AI literacy and ethics training for instructional designers and educators. We can foster a culture of responsible and ethical innovation in instructional design by building a shared understanding of AI technologies' capabilities, limitations, and potential risks. This could involve the creation of guidelines, best practices, and standards for using AI in education, as well as ongoing professional development opportunities for instructional designers to stay up-to-date with the latest developments and considerations in the field.

Ultimately, the future of AI in instructional design is one of immense possibility and potential. By leveraging the power of AI to create more personalized, engaging, and effective learning experiences, instructional designers can transform how we learn and grow throughout our lives. However, realizing this potential will require ongoing collaboration, experimentation, and dialogue among instructional designers, educators, learners, and other stakeholders. Only by working together can we ensure that the future of AI-powered learning benefits and empowers all learners, regardless of their backgrounds or circumstances.

As we look ahead to this exciting future, there are countless opportunities for instructional designers to lead the way in shaping the direction and impact of AI in education. Whether through the creation of innovative AI-powered learning solutions, the development of new frameworks and methodologies for AI-driven instructional design, or the advancement of research and thought leadership in the field, instructional designers have a vital role to play in ensuring that the future of learning harnesses the power of AI for the benefit of all.

So, let us embrace this challenge with enthusiasm, creativity, and a deep commitment to education's transformative potential. By staying curious, collaborating openly, and always putting learners' needs first, we can create a compelling, efficient, equitable, empowering, and endlessly inspiring future of AI-powered instructional design.

9. Conclusion

Throughout this book, we have explored the vast and exciting landscape of artificial intelligence in instructional design. We have seen how AI technologies transform how we create, deliver, and evaluate learning experiences, from personalized learning paths and adaptive assessments to virtual tutors and immersive simulations. We have considered the many benefits and opportunities AI offers learners, educators, and instructional designers alike, as well as the challenges and considerations of integrating AI into education.

As we have discovered, the story of AI in instructional design has immense potential and possibility. By leveraging the power of machine learning, natural language processing, and other AI technologies, instructional designers can create learning experiences that are more engaging, effective, and tailored to each learner's unique needs and goals. We have seen how AI can help us scale and optimize education's impact, reaching learners across geographic and demographic boundaries with high-quality, data-driven instruction.

At the same time, we have grappled with AI's complex ethical and social implications in education. We have considered the risks of algorithmic bias and the importance of ensuring that AI-powered learning experiences are designed with fairness, transparency, and accountability in mind. We have emphasized the need for human judgment and oversight in using AI, recognizing that while AI can augment and enhance human capabilities, it cannot replace the creativity, empathy, and contextual understanding that skilled instructional designers bring to their work.

Throughout our exploration, we have been guided by the stories and experiences of instructional designers like Sofia, who have embraced the potential of AI to create transformative learning experiences. Through fictional case studies and future-focused vignettes, we have seen how instructional designers already use AI to personalize learning, streamline workflows, and gain new insights into learner behavior and performance. We have been inspired by their creativity, passion, and commitment to leveraging technology to enhance learner success and well-being.

As we look to the future of AI in instructional design, the possibilities are vast and unpredictable. We can imagine a world where AI-powered learning experiences are the norm, where learners can access high-quality, personalized instruction anytime, anywhere, and on any device. We can envision a future where instructional designers collaborate closely with AI systems, leveraging data and algorithms to create real-time learning experiences that adapt to learner needs and preferences. We can imagine a future where AI helps us to bridge the gaps between education and the rapidly changing world of work, providing learners with the skills and competencies they need to thrive in an age of accelerating technological change.

At the same time, we must approach this future with a critical eye and a commitment to ethical and responsible innovation. We must prioritize the development of AI literacy and ethics training for instructional designers and educators, ensuring that we have the knowledge and frameworks needed to use AI in ways that benefit and empower all learners. We must foster ongoing dialogue and collaboration among diverse stakeholders – including learners, educators, policymakers, and technology developers – to ensure that a broad range of perspectives and experiences shapes the future of AI in education.

Ultimately, the story of AI in instructional design is still being written, and its ending is up to us. As instructional designers, educators, and lifelong learners, we have the opportunity—and the responsibility—to shape the direction and impact of AI in education. By staying curious, critical, and committed to technology's transformative potential, we can create a future of learning that is more engaging, effective, and equitable than ever before.

So, let us embrace this challenge with open minds and hearts, ready to learn from the past, experiment in the present, and imagine the future. Let us continue to push the boundaries of what is possible with AI and instructional design, always keeping the needs and dreams of learners at the center of our work. And let us never lose sight of the incredible privilege and potential we have as educators and designers to shape the minds and lives of learners across the globe.

We are creating the future of AI-powered instructional design, and I cannot wait to see what we will achieve together.

About the Author

Ruchir Bakshi is a seasoned instructional systems designer with over two decades of experience creating engaging and effective learning solutions for private and government organizations. Based in Columbia, MD, Ruchir brings knowledge, expertise, and passion to his work, consistently delivering innovative and impactful instructional designs.

Throughout his impressive career, Ruchir has honed his skills in various aspects of instructional design, staying at the forefront of the ever-evolving field. His keen interest in Artificial Intelligence and its applications in instructional design has enabled him to incorporate cutting-edge techniques and tools into his design process, ensuring that his learning solutions are both practical and future-proof. This book, "Unleashing AI: Harnessing the Power of Artificial Intelligence in Instructional Design," is a testament to Ruchir's deep understanding of the subject matter and his ability to present complex concepts in an accessible and engaging manner.

In the book, Ruchir introduces a recurring fictional scenario that follows the journey of an instructional designer named Sofia as she navigates the challenges and opportunities of AI-powered instructional design. Through Sofia's experiences, readers gain a deeper understanding of how AI can be applied in real-world contexts and are inspired to think creatively about the potential of AI in their work.

As a consultant, Ruchir brings his unique blend of instructional design expertise, technological savvy, and social awareness to help organizations navigate complex challenges and create meaningful change. His confident, analytical approach and empathetic, respectful communication style make him a sought-after expert.

Beyond his work in instructional design, Ruchir is a passionate advocate for various social causes. He is a strong proponent of mental health awareness, using his platform to break down stigmas and promote understanding and support for those facing mental health challenges. Ruchir's commitment to this cause is evident in his writing and tireless efforts to spread awareness and encourage open dialogue.

Ruchir's diverse interests and pursuits reflect his dedication to lifelong learning. When he's not designing innovative learning solutions, Ruchir can be found studying a wide range of subjects, from advancements in instructional design to the intricacies of human rights and racism. His thirst for knowledge and understanding drives him to expand his expertise and continuously share his insights with others.

As a combat veteran, Ruchir has served multiple deployments in Afghanistan, Iraq, and other locations under Operations Enduring Freedom and Iraqi Freedom. His experiences have shaped his perspective and instilled in him a strong sense of dedication, resilience, and adaptability – qualities he brings to his work as an instructional designer. Despite the challenges he has faced, including his struggle with PTSD resulting from his combat exposure, Ruchir has channeled his experiences into a driving force for positive change, both in his professional and personal life.

In "Unleashing AI," Ruchir invites readers to join him on a transformative journey through AI-powered instructional design. With his authoritative yet engaging tone, Ruchir guides readers through AI's practical applications and potential in creating tailored, effective, and truly transformative learning experiences. His wealth of knowledge and passion for innovation and social responsibility make this book an essential resource for instructional designers, educators, and anyone interested in the future of learning.

Made in United States
Orlando, FL
05 August 2024